MW00935450

Introduction

I created this book because I was tired of reading the same advice

from websites and books. This book of advice comes from experi-

ences of my own. I am no expert in the field of healthcare, childcare,

or pregnancy, just a new mommy like you.

I hope you enjoy reading and find my 101 tips & tricks helpful!

Visit the hospital before delivery, so you are comfortable with your surroundings. This includes taking a few practice runs, to make sure you know where to go for

delivery.

Complete the nursery at least a month in advance.

Install the car seat early, in case baby comes early. It's a pain to have to worry about installing it while at the hospital.

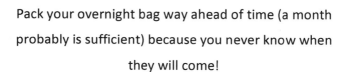

Pack your overnight bag way ahead of time (a month probably is sufficient) because you never know when they will come!

Pack for three days of clothing. You may be more comfortable wearing the hospital gown the whole time, but this is just in case you want your clothes. Pack for about the size you were at 6 months pregnant, but obviously you can pack for when you were 9 months.

Pack sports bras. They are super comfy for delivery, and while recovering for a few days in hospital.

Most birthing rooms will have a DVD player, so pack some DVD's and throw in your overnight bag. You could be in labor for only a few minutes, or even a day and a half for new mommies.

Buy a few preemie outfits. You may THINK your baby is a certain weight, or won't come early, but you will need them if they come early. Don't buy too many, in case you don't get to use them at all. Try a 2nd hand store, since they are usually super cheap there.

Second hand stores are great for baby clothes, maternity clothes, and even baby toys! Don't feel like you are being cheap by not buying new items, think of it as saving money. Why not get a pair of maternity jeans for $7 instead of $40+ brand new?

Cook big meals ahead of time and freeze them. It is so convenient to have already made meals, because you may not have the time to cook, or the energy, once baby comes.

Call your insurance company in advance and ask what they cover for delivery, and for new baby doctor visits. If you don't have insurance, talk to your OB/GYN about what the cost will be to you for all of your prenatal visits and delivery.

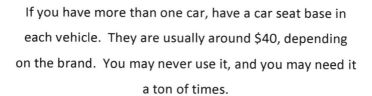

If you have more than one car, have a car seat base in each vehicle. They are usually around $40, depending on the brand. You may never use it, and you may need it a ton of times.

Call your insurance company to see if a new breast pump is covered. Some even will cover it 100%.

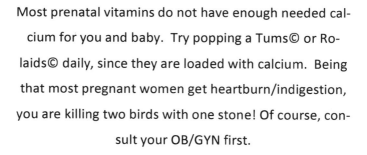

Most prenatal vitamins do not have enough needed calcium for you and baby. Try popping a Tums© or Ro-
laids© daily, since they are loaded with calcium. Being
that most pregnant women get heartburn/indigestion,
you are killing two birds with one stone! Of course, consult your OB/GYN first.

Join thebump.com ©– The site has message boards where other pregnant women and mommies post advice and ask each other questions. It's super helpful, and fun to read! My suggestion is when joining, not to create an obvious username, like your first and last name. Once you create it you cannot change it.

Make sure to buy a large pack of sanitary napkins (pads) for after a vaginal delivery. You will get some at the hospital, but will go through them like crazy at home. You will need them for at least the first week or longer.

Start a library for your baby early. We hit garage sales, second hand stores, and even libraries and had a complete bookcase filled for less than $60 before baby came!

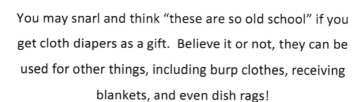

You may snarl and think "these are so old school" if you get cloth diapers as a gift. Believe it or not, they can be used for other things, including burp clothes, receiving blankets, and even dish rags!

If you receive baby shower gifts that you want to return, but don't have a receipt, don't feel bad to ask the person where they got it. Sometimes you can tell from the tag where it was purchased. If not, re-gift it. If you feel guilty, throw it in as something additional, not the main gift.

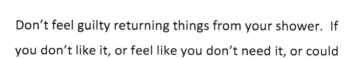

Don't feel guilty returning things from your shower. If you don't like it, or feel like you don't need it, or could use something else more, then do it!

Yes, it is normal to stalk your online registry to see what people have purchased...even as early as the day after you send out the invites ☺

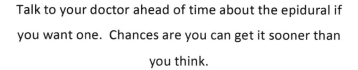

Talk to your doctor ahead of time about the epidural if
you want one. Chances are you can get it sooner than
you think.

Read up about Jaundice before delivery, because it's normal for newborns to have.

Don't go overboard on newborn shoes, because chances are they will be living in onesies for months.

A will or a trust should be in place before baby comes.

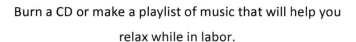

Burn a CD or make a playlist of music that will help you relax while in labor.

Register, or spend the money for a good monitor you really like – ITS WORTH IT!

In your overnight bag, pack snacks that you like. Hospital food is not always the yummiest.

Not everybody's water breaks. So don't expect this to
be the first sign of labor.

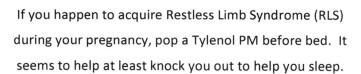

If you happen to acquire Restless Limb Syndrome (RLS) during your pregnancy, pop a Tylenol PM before bed. It seems to help at least knock you out to help you sleep. As always, consult with your Doctor first.

Keep a journal of the events that led up to birth so you can look back.

If you don't have all of the supplies you need at the hospital, don't worry, they should have EVERYTHING the baby will need.

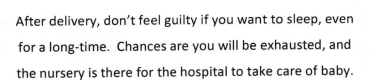

After delivery, don't feel guilty if you want to sleep, even for a long-time. Chances are you will be exhausted, and the nursery is there for the hospital to take care of baby.

Keep baby in the hospital nursery when you want to take a nap, or take a shower. Don't let them make you feel guilty for not having you baby in the room with you at all times. Even if its 2pm, or 2am in the morning.

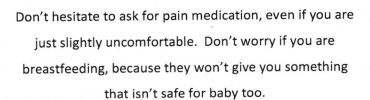

Don't hesitate to ask for pain medication, even if you are just slightly uncomfortable. Don't worry if you are breastfeeding, because they won't give you something that isn't safe for baby too.

Confirm with your nurse first, but you should be able to take whatever hospital supplies (pads, underwear), and baby supplies that come in your babies portable crib cart. You're insurance, or you, are paying for these, and they are handy in case you don't already have a diaper bag packed before you leave the hospital.

If you are not being monitored on an I.V., are feeling fine, and baby is doing fine, you can probably leave the hospital sooner than you think! Confirm with a nurse, but you don't have to wait around for someone to tell you that you can leave.

If experiencing long labor and you are having a vaginal delivery, they will probably want you to empty your bladder to make room for baby. There are two ways to do this: bedpan, or catheter. If you have an epidural the catheter isn't as bad as it sounds.

Don't worry if you didn't take Lamaze classes. You will learn to breathe at the hospital.

Ask a nurse or your partner to put a "Do Not Disturb" sign on your hospital door if you are trying to get some rest. You need to regain your strength after going through delivery!

Why not donate your cord blood if you aren't banking it?

It's FREE, and otherwise they'd just be throwing it away.

Ask your nurse to change your positions during labor if you are uncomfortable or are not dilating as much as they want you to. If can make a world of difference and even speed up delivery.

Don't hesitate to ask for a break during labor if you've been pushing for a long time. I personally pushed for three hours, got a 3 contraction break, and was able to push him out fifteen minutes later. All I needed was to regain my strength.

Visitors will be eager to visit, especially the day of or day after delivery. Don't hesitate to just tell them you'll call them later when you wake up.

Chances are, if you didn't have an enema, or had solid food within 12 hours of delivery, you will go #2 while in labor.

Don't worry; the squishy tummy is completely normal after delivery!

Immediately after delivery (and for me several hours after) you can see your abdomen literally jumping by itself. This is your uterus contracting to stop the bleeding and trying to get back to its original shape.

When getting wheeled out of the hospital (you don't have to), make sure to have a blanket over your baby, because people can bombard you to see baby. It sounds cute, but it can get annoying.

Put a clock in the rooms you are in most often. You'll constantly be looking for what time it is due to scheduled feedings/diaper changes.

Create a spreadsheet on paper, for when you feed baby and to record diaper changes. The first week is crucial for this especially, because the Doctor will ask you how often baby is eating and having pee/poopy diapers.

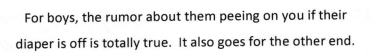

For boys, the rumor about them peeing on you if their diaper is off is totally true. It also goes for the other end.

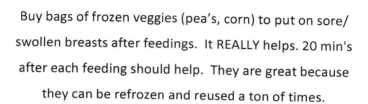

Buy bags of frozen veggies (pea's, corn) to put on sore/ swollen breasts after feedings. It REALLY helps. 20 min's after each feeding should help. They are great because they can be refrozen and reused a ton of times.

Nap when they nap – You'll read this everywhere, but it is so true and will pay off. You might have to find techniques that work for you to fall asleep in the middle of the day, but it's worth it.

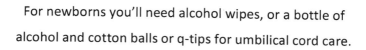

For newborns you'll need alcohol wipes, or a bottle of alcohol and cotton balls or q-tips for umbilical cord care.

Buy baby band-aids. They fit and stay much better than regular band-aids.

If you have a pack-n-play with an attached changing station, make sure to keep it stocked with all diapering supplies, and a change of outfit. I also put receiving blankets and bibs in mine, so I had everything at my fingertips immediately.

You will likely go through about 12 diapers a day. So calculate that when buying diapers. You'd rather have too many, than too little, so you don't have to worry about running to the store.

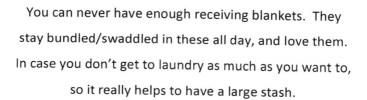

You can never have enough receiving blankets. They stay bundled/swaddled in these all day, and love them. In case you don't get to laundry as much as you want to, so it really helps to have a large stash.

Don't feel guilty if you can't fill out your baby book as much as you want. We jotted down "firsts" and "visitors" in a notebook and you can always transfer these things later. Or keep a pile of keepsakes, like your hospital bracelet and the babies and worry about putting together later.

Keep a camera close; you will always want it for cute pictures. This goes for video cameras too.

Remind visitors to wash hands before holding baby and return when healthy if they are sick.

Have medical masks on-hand, in case someone has a cough and wants to hold baby. You can buy these usually at any place with a pharmacy. Tell them they can take the mask off for pictures, but it needs to go right back on.

Before every baby visit, jot down any question you can think of, it is what they are there for. Don't rely on the internet/friends for answers, and always call the doctor with any concerns.

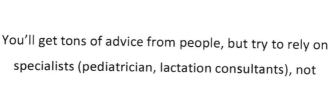

You'll get tons of advice from people, but try to rely on specialists (pediatrician, lactation consultants), not friends and family. Everybody will tell you something different based on THEIR experience, but you could have a totally different experience.

Extra visitors the first few days may exhaust you more than you think, but they are nice to have for you to take a nap.

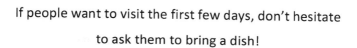

If people want to visit the first few days, don't hesitate to ask them to bring a dish!

When buying baby clothes, make sure to buy appropri-
ate to the season. If they are born in summer, you'll
want more short-sleeved/legged outfits than all long-
sleeved/legged outfits. You don't want your baby to
overheat or sweat all day.

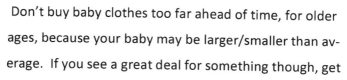

Don't buy baby clothes too far ahead of time, for older ages, because your baby may be larger/smaller than average. If you see a great deal for something though, get it!

Mom-to-Mom sales are amazing. You can get expensive items for a steal!

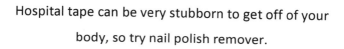

Hospital tape can be very stubborn to get off of your body, so try nail polish remover.

Take a shower, eat, and do an errand around the house as soon as baby falls asleep. Sometimes you can have a few hours, or a few minutes to do things, so take advantage of the time that you have.

Take advantage of getting to do things for you when visitors come. Of course only if they are comfortable being around baby alone and you trust your baby with them.

Be sure to have formula on hand, in case you have trouble breastfeeding or pumping. You'll hear from professionals that most mommies' milk does not come in for a few days.

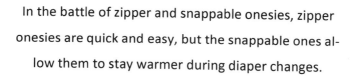

In the battle of zipper and snappable onesies, zipper onesies are quick and easy, but the snappable ones allow them to stay warmer during diaper changes.

Formula may seem expensive, but keep in mind that this is the ONLY thing baby is eating or drinking! My experience is that the smaller eight oz. canisters last only a few days; the 23.4 oz. ones about a week (this is based on 2-3oz feedings.)

You'll read everywhere that most babies eat/sleep every two-three hours, but my experience is it can be even 45 minutes or an hour, so be prepared! Don't assume baby isn't hungry even if they just ate a little bit ago.

If you have lots of people wanting pictures, snap-fish.com© is a great place to use to upload/email albums/order prints.

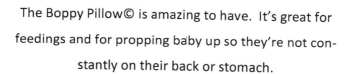

The Boppy Pillow© is amazing to have. It's great for feedings and for propping baby up so they're not con-stantly on their back or stomach.

Invest in baby fingernail clippers. Their nails grow fast and they can easily scratch their face with them. This helps if they can't seem to keep mittens on.

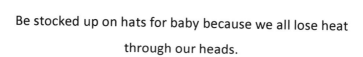

Be stocked up on hats for baby because we all lose heat through our heads.

If you have a boy, and get him circumcised, you'll need petroleum jelly at home to put on his penis so it doesn't stick to the diaper. The doctor that performs the procedure or the pediatrician should tell you for how long. You'll also need it for taking a rectal temperature.

Make sure to have baby lotion on hand, because after a bath their skin can get extremely dry.

You'll hear "no blankets in the crib", but that doesn't mean they can't be tightly swaddled in a receiving blanket. Of course consult with your pediatrician first.

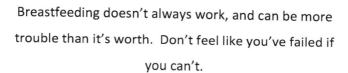

Breastfeeding doesn't always work, and can be more trouble than it's worth. Don't feel like you've failed if you can't.

Get a microwavable bottle steamer. It's a quick way to sterilize your bottles, nipples, pacifiers, and bottle caps.

Don't hesitate to tell family and friends to stop doing
something, you don't like around the baby: You are
baby's protector.

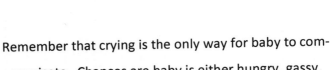

Remember that crying is the only way for baby to communicate. Chances are baby is either hungry, gassy, cold, needs a diaper change, or even wants to be held. Of course other things could be wrong, but these seem to be the most common.

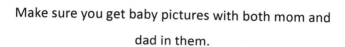

Make sure you get baby pictures with both mom and dad in them.

I highly recommend buying Mylicon drops© for gas. It is safe for every feeding (per the box) and is pediatrician recommended!

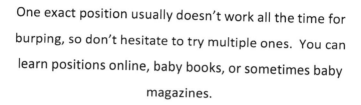

One exact position usually doesn't work all the time for burping, so don't hesitate to try multiple ones. You can learn positions online, baby books, or sometimes baby magazines.

In the debate of using a pacifier, I choose no pacifier! It becomes mommy & daddy's job to replace it when it falls out, which can be every few minutes. This can get extremely tiring after awhile; especially in the middle of the night.

For Him

Allow him to be a part of the pregnancy process.

Invite him to be in the delivery room, and to help out. Helping out can be anything from getting you juice, calling the nurse, or rubbing your back during contractions. Just make him feel a part of it!

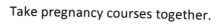

Take pregnancy courses together.

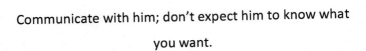

Communicate with him; don't expect him to know what you want.

Have him keep the family updated as much as he can, but don't let them allow him feel guilty if they don't get an update when they want one. He is busy with baby and mommy!

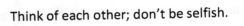

Think of each other; don't be selfish.

Work as a team. Things will run MUCH smoother!

Discuss, in advance, how much time he needs to take off work to help out after delivery.

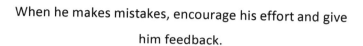

When he makes mistakes, encourage his effort and give him feedback.

86854989R00057

Made in the USA
Lexington, KY
16 April 2018